FiDDLE RHyTHMS

by SALLY O'REiLLY

ISBN 0-8497-5715-0

©1992 **Neil A. Kjos Music Company,** 4380 Jutland Drive, San Diego, California, 92117.
International copyright secured. All rights reserved. Printed in U. S. A.
Warning! All the music, text, and art in this book are protected by copyright law.
To copy or reproduce them by any method is an infringement of the copyright law.
Anyone who reproduces copyrighted matter is subject to substantial penalties and assessments for each infringement.

kjos Neil A. Kjos Music Company • San Diego, California

INTRODUCTION

During my many years as a teacher, I have learned the value of word association in teaching accurate rhythmic concepts to students of all ages.

I recommend the following order of practice:
1. Clap the rhythm with the metronome set at ♩ = 60.
2. Play the rhythmic figure repeatedly on an open string with the metronome set at ♩ = 60.
3. Play the study as written.

By separating the element of rhythm from the problems of coordinating the left hand with the right arm we strengthen the drive of a piece. Because rhythm is the *backbone* of music, it is essential that students develop total command of the rhythmic vocabulary.

I hope both students and teachers enjoy working in *Fiddle Rhythms* as much as I enjoyed writing it!

Sally O'Reilly

APPLES

I Like Apple Pie

Melody
Rubinstein

Theme From Haydn's "Surprise" Symphony
Haydn

This Old Man
Folk Song

HUCKLEBERRY

I Like Huckleberry Pie

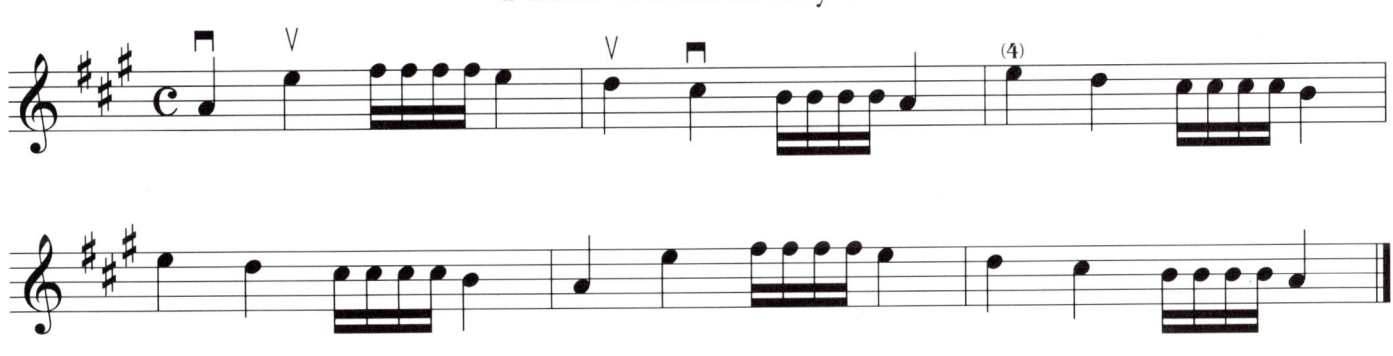

Shortnin' Bread

Moderato ♩=72

Folk Song

Hornpipe

Allegro

Sailors Song

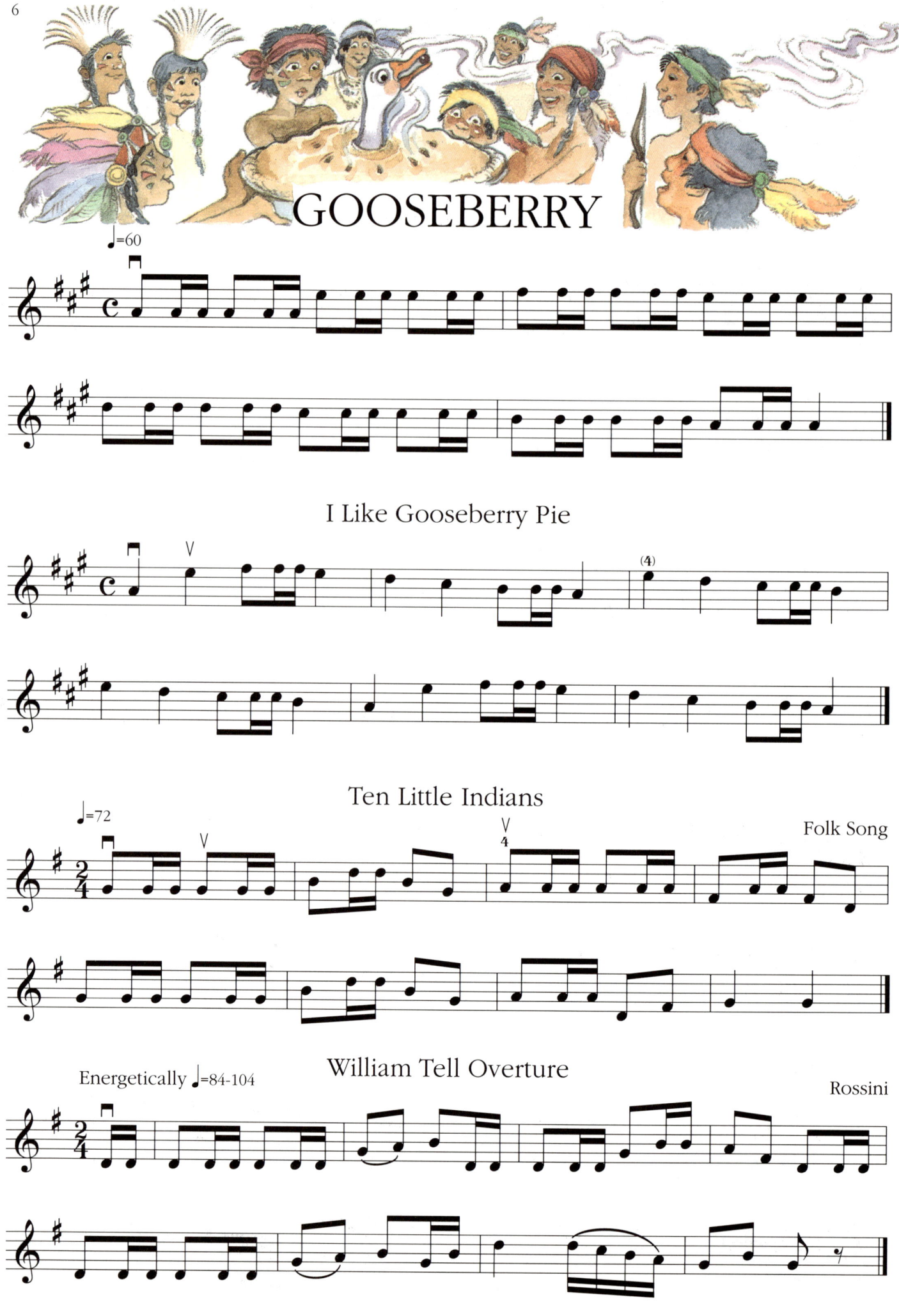

PIZZA

Bowing Variations

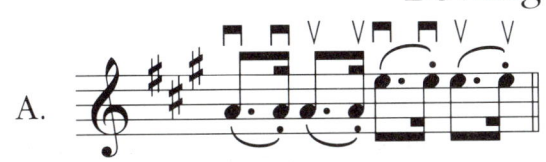

A.

B.

(At tip of bow)

I Like Pizza Pie

Scottish Air

O'Reilly

The Marriage Of Figaro

Allegro

Mozart

BANANA

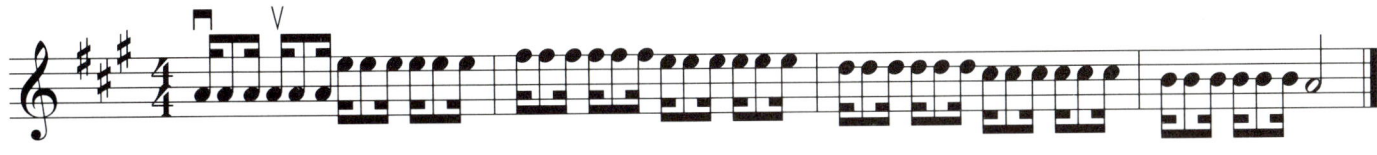

I Like Banana Pie

Fiddle Tango

O'Reilly

The Banana Boat

O'Reilly

Nobody Knows The Trouble I've Seen

Spiritual

PUMPKIN

I Like Pumpkin Pie

The Mulberry Bush
Folk Song

Fiddle-Dee-Dee
Rossini
fine

D.C. al fine

Pop! Goes The Weasel
Folk Song

VANILLA

(L.H.)

I Like Vanilla Pie

Toccata
Kabalevsky

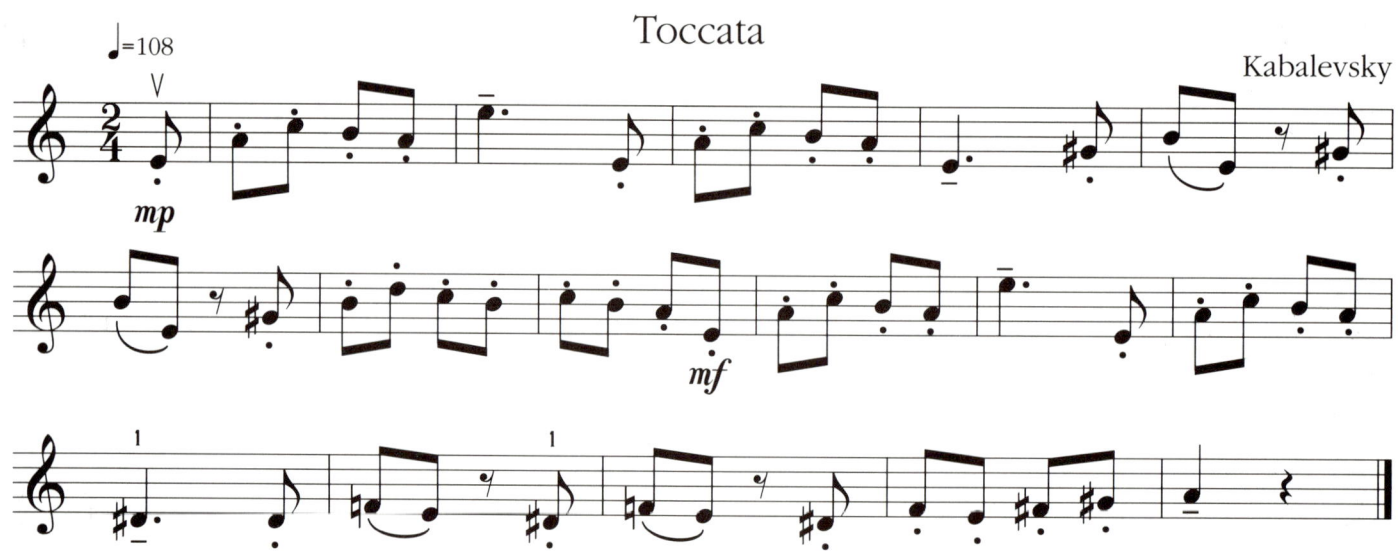

Andantino
Campagnoli

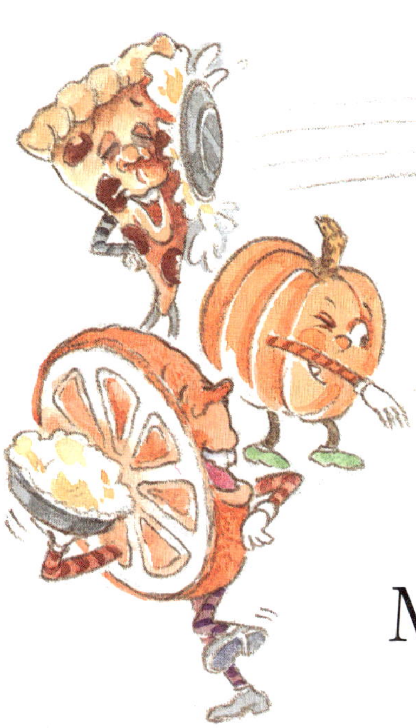

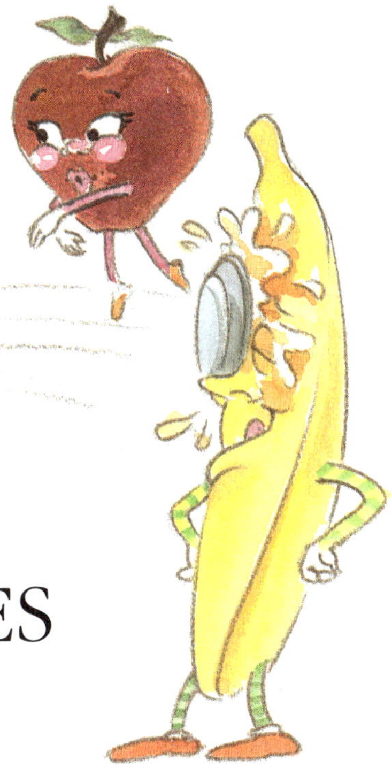

MORE MIXED PIES

Russian Theme

Tchaikovsky

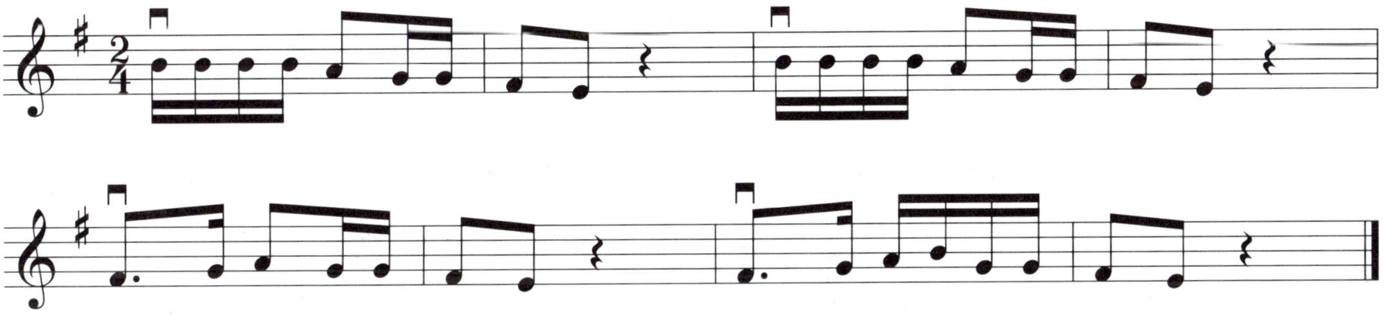

Melody

Moderato ♩=72-84

Purcell

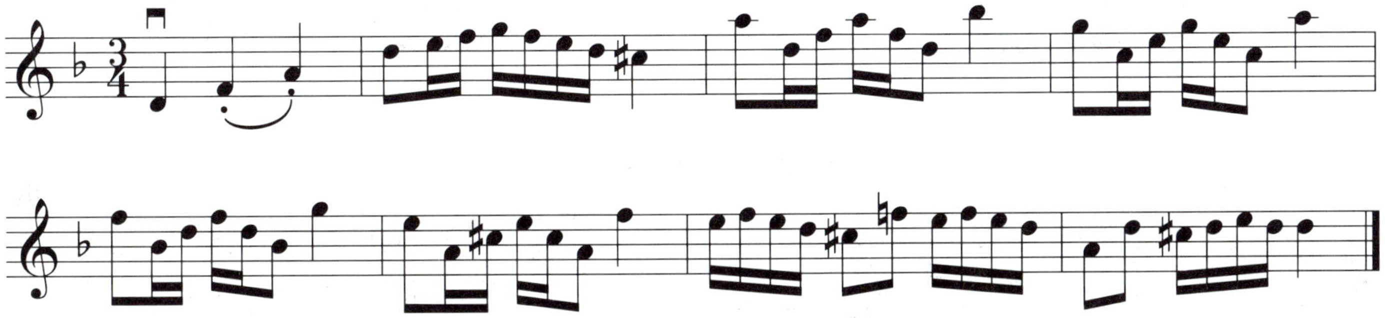

Waltz From "Swan Lake"

Tchaikovsky

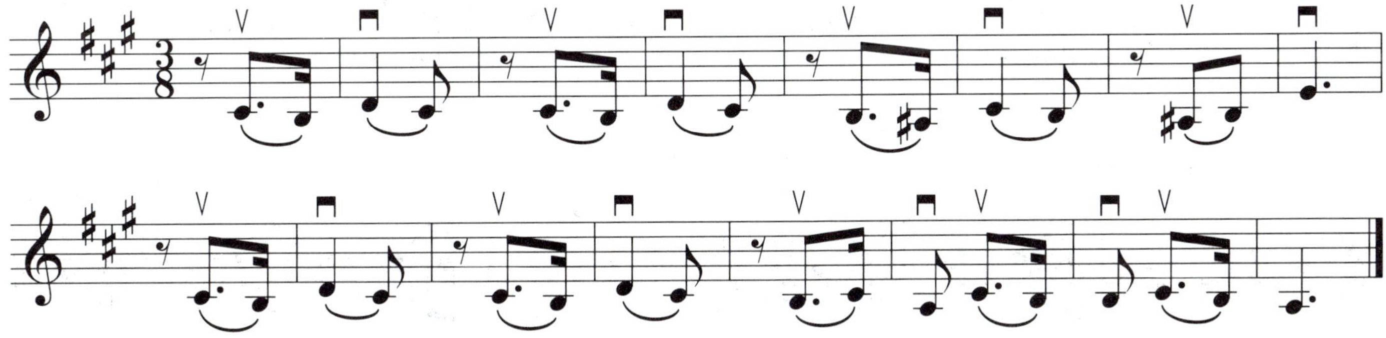

March From "The Nutcracker"
Tchaikovsky

Robin Adair
Scottish Air

Cantabile
Haydn

Andante ♪=108

QUIZ

1. Identify the following pies:

   a.  _____   g.  _____

   b.  _____   h.  _____

   c.  _____   i.  _____

   d.  _____   j.  _____

   e.  _____   k.  _____

   f.  _____   l. _____

2. Name the pies that "fill" a quarter note:

   a. _____   e. _____

   b. _____   f. _____

   c. _____   g. _____

   d. _____

3. Write four measures in 4/4 using seven different pies:

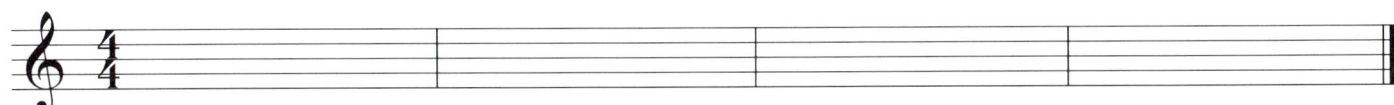

4. Write four measures in 6/8 using four different pies:

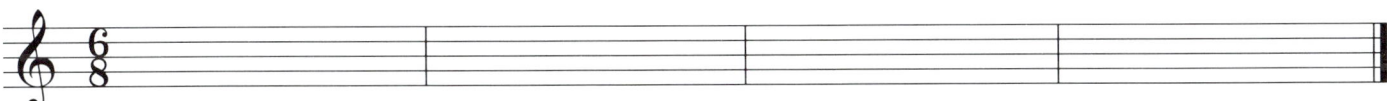

5. Clap and count aloud each of the above exercises (♩=60).

6. Play each of the above exercises on an open string (♩=60).